A PLACE CALLED
THE COLORED CAR

A PLACE CALLED THE COLORED CAR

REGINALD F. SMITH, SR.

A PLACE CALLED THE COLORED CAR

Copyright © 2019 Reginald F. Smith, Sr.

All rights reserved. No part of this book may be used or reproduced by any means, graphic, electronic, or mechanical, including photocopying, recording, taping or by any information storage retrieval system without the written permission of the author except in the case of brief quotations embodied in critical articles and reviews.

iUniverse books may be ordered through booksellers or by contacting:

iUniverse
1663 Liberty Drive
Bloomington, IN 47403
www.iuniverse.com
1-800-Authors (1-800-288-4677)

Because of the dynamic nature of the Internet, any web addresses or links contained in this book may have changed since publication and may no longer be valid. The views expressed in this work are solely those of the author and do not necessarily reflect the views of the publisher, and the publisher hereby disclaims any responsibility for them.

Any people depicted in stock imagery provided by Getty Images are models, and such images are being used for illustrative purposes only. Certain stock imagery © Getty Images.

ISBN: 978-1-5320-8235-1 (sc)
ISBN: 978-1-5320-8236-8 (e)

Library of Congress Control Number: 2019914364

Print information available on the last page.

iUniverse rev. date: 09/25/2019

CONTENTS

1. Acknowledgments vii
2. Introduction ix
3. Early to Rise 1
4. Sunday at our house 7
5. A Visit from {My Uncle} 11
6. Going to visit {My Uncle} 19
7. The Train Ride to Chicago 25
8. So Glad to See {My Uncle} 37
9. Author's Bio 45

ACKNOWLEDGMENTS

This book is dedicated to my greatest blessings and inspiration, my family. My mother Shirley, loving wife Jacquelyn and two children Reginald II and Regina. And my ancestors, without their sacrifices this book would not have been made possible.

"You can never know where you are going unless you know where you have been." — Amelia Boynton Robinson

INTRODUCTION

How Could We?

A Place Called the Colored Car tells the story of Sam, a bright, happy, 10-year-old boy and his epic train ride from Memphis, Tennessee to Chicago, Illinois in the mid-1950s. Sam was born and raised in Memphis and lived

with his mother, Ruth, his grandmother, Beth and his grandfather, Elijah.

The racial injustices experienced on that trip were so horrible and so alarming that even through a child's eyes, you can see, feel, hear, taste, smell and cry for what people had to endure simply because God blessed them with dark skin. We witness human beings being treated less than our worst imaginable nightmares. The book forces the question we should all ask: "How *Could* We?"

EARLY TO RISE

Everybody in our house played a part in getting ready for the day. Grandmother was in the kitchen stirring the oatmeal. Biscuits were baking in the oven and bacon was sizzling on the stove. The smells wafting through the house were so beautiful it made me want to get up and shout! Getting up early was easy when I knew Grandmother was in the kitchen.

And if I was lucky I would sometimes get a little milk and a pinch of sugar in my oatmeal. Grandmother knew this little spoonful of sweetness would make me smile, so maybe once or twice a week she made sure there was something extra to smile about. I loved my grandmother so much!

Grandfather was busy doing whatever it was that grandfathers do. To this day I still don't know exactly

what my granddaddy did. I knew he was somehow connected to the distribution of the city's two Black-owned newspapers and because of him, many people had jobs. But if he had an important title, he never told me about it. All I knew was that my granddaddy was the lifeblood of our household.

Granddaddy always made sure the lights were turned on and turned off to "save electricity." He made sure we had food to eat and that the grass was cut. He and my grandmother fed the chickens in our backyard and tended to a vegetable garden that produced much of what was on our plates each evening. Granddaddy always encouraged us to do better and he made sure we all had a reason to smile.

My mom was a fifth-grade school teacher. Mama's entire focus, Monday through Friday, was getting to work and getting me to school. We always left the house early so she could make sure I got to school safe and sound. From the time I pushed open the school door with an armful of books and writing pads, until the time the dismissal bell rang, I knew there was only one task—one job—that was more important than anything else. It was my responsibility to learn something of value for that day. This was my job, *every* school day!

Each morning began with our heads bowed as we prayed the Lord's Prayer. Someone from the class would then be chosen to read a verse from the Bible. I was always happy when my teacher picked me. Then, with our hands over our hearts, we recited the Pledge of Allegiance. I wasn't really sure what all those words meant, but they

made me feel proud to be an American. Liberty and justice sounded very serious and important, and I couldn't help but think those words applied to me.

Next up was a review of the ABC's, and that's how we began every school day. School was of great importance to my family, my family was very important to me, this made school one of the most important things in my life.

SUNDAY AT OUR HOUSE

In my grandmother and grandfather's house, Sunday, the Lord's Day was the best day of the week. I was allowed to wear my best pair of pants, nicest shirt, my grown-up looking tie, and my good lace-up shoes, which I always shined the night before. I loved the feeling of wearing my Sunday clothes.

I owned two pair of pants; one for school, which mom washed out and rung dry each night, and then carefully hung over the floor furnace to dry. My other pair was my Sunday pants, only to be worn on the Lord's Day and other special occasions.

Sunday rituals seldom changed. First, we attended Sunday school, then the 10:00 AM church service. Later that evening we returned for the Young People Willing Workers (YPWW) meeting. This group was one that

performed services in our community, such as raking the leaves for our elderly neighbors, or carrying over food to someone's house if they needed it. We also learned and studied the Bible.

Our entire day revolved around our church, and it was here I learned the foundations of respect, honesty and the dignity of work.

My grandfather, grandmother, and my mother lived by these unquestioning principles, and so did I.

Inside the COGIC sanctuary, it was warm and inviting with the smell of wooden pews and the faint scent of the lilacs adorning the altar. Fans and hymn books were scattered on the seats of the pews. I always watched as the ushers made sure everybody was comfortably seated, and that no one was chewing gum or slouching. I knew it was their job to see no one was napping and that everyone was paying attention to the preacher.

Sundays will always remain present in my childhood memories. I will always remember how my grandmother invited our family members from all over the neighborhood to come to her house to eat and visit. There was talk, laughter, and fun. But there was one important rule: A child stayed in a child's place. I was not allowed to take part in any of the adult's conversations.

A VISIT FROM MY UNCLE

My Uncle Joe was my mother's older brother, and he lived in Chicago, Illinois. My uncle would come and visit us maybe twice a year. I remember it was always such a fantastic occasion! It was like my birthday, Christmas, and the 4th of July all rolled into one. Could anyone even *imagine*? It was like having all the cakes, toys and candy in the world and it was all *mine*! When Uncle Joe came to visit, the feeling, the anticipation, and the joy were almost unbearable.

His visits always included something special for me. I knew whatever my uncle brought me was going to be awesome. It might be a toy, it could be a piece of clothing, it could even be a stick from his yard. It didn't matter! The only thing that *did* matter was that everybody in my family was going to be happy. I knew my mother, my

grandmother and my grandfather would also share in my happiness. It gave me an intense, indescribable glow to see our house radiate with joy.

My uncle's visit brought other special delights. There was going to be plenty of delicious food to eat. There would be roast beef, fried chicken, mashed potatoes, coleslaw, string beans, rolls, we even had cakes and pies. Granddaddy would slaughter a chicken or two from our backyard and I knew there would be a drive to Hernando, Mississippi where he'd buy pork sausage and fresh beef for the roast. Mama would visit the local sundry to purchase other ingredients like shredded coconut for one of her delicious pies.

But greater than the gifts from Chicago and all the tasty food my grandmother would cook, there was a special bond shared by me and my uncle. We spent many lengthy afternoons together and we'd talk about everything. He told me things no one, not even Mom or my teachers, ever told me. He explained why a blade of grass was green, how butterflies emerged from cocoons and why cars needed batteries to run. It seemed as though my uncle knew everything. During these special times, I always felt safe, loved and secure. I was reassured that my uncle shared with me all the answers to the world's biggest secrets.

At this time in my young life, my uncle's love meant more to me than anyone could ever imagine. His presence filled every room and was like a breath of fresh air. I watched Uncle Joe as he carefully combed his thick black hair, just so. I watched him eat, I tried to memorize how

he lifted his fork and dabbed at the corner of his mouth with a napkin. I even tried to sit like him and walk as he did. I dreamed that one day I'd be just like Uncle Joe.

While in Memphis, he took me with him to the barbershop, to the shoeshine shop and the newspaper stand. We'd walk down Beale Street together and I felt like the most important boy in the world. He took time with me to do things no one else ever did. He always knew the right things to say, and whenever I had a doubt about anything, I knew when I was with my uncle he would have the right answer.

Uncle Joe wanted to know things like, "What do you plan to be when you grow up?" I would puzzle my brain for a response that would please him. No one else ever asked me questions like this, or seemingly even cared. I told him I planned to be a fireman. He'd say, "A fireman is good but when I show up to the fire station, you better be the fire chief!" His words thrilled me, and my mind would suddenly fill with visions of shiny red firetrucks, large blazing fires and I could see myself all grownup and directing people around me. I felt heroic and invincible!

Often Uncle Joe took me somewhere unexpectedly nice. One time we walked into the lobby of the Peabody Hotel. He told me this was the finest hotel in all of the South, and he instructed me to look at the beauty of the architecture. I was amazed at the grandeur—the sparkling chandeliers, the marble floors, huge vases of flowers everywhere. Someone was playing a piano softly while admiring guests gathered around to watch. Beautiful Persian rugs adorned the floor and everyone seemed to

be well dressed and happy. There was a gigantic fountain in the middle of the lobby, and I was shocked to see ducks swimming in the water like they belonged there. "Yes, they do live here," said Uncle Joe with a smile. I told him I never heard of ducks living in a hotel.

Moments later I saw my uncle slip five dollars to a uniformed man who worked there. I didn't question it because it was my uncle. Later I found out he paid the man to let me be the guest duck master for that afternoon. I didn't know it at the time, but it was against the rules for me to be a guest duck master because of the color of my skin. But he wanted me to have that experience. We walked into the fancy elevator with the duck master and with the Peabody ducks, cooing and trilling around our feet.

When we reached the rooftop I led the waddling troop of ducks off the elevator. I marched in front of them ceremoniously, and for a brief time, *I* was the Peabody duck master! When I was with my uncle I felt as though there was nothing I could not do.

When it was time for my uncle to return to Chicago, I cried. I didn't want anyone to see me, so I hid in the bathroom. But I was there to hug him and wave goodbye. It was a sad time for me when my uncle left to go back home.

GOING TO VISIT MY UNCLE

One Saturday we were sitting in the living room and grandmother announced, "We should take Sam to Chicago to visit his uncle Joe." I had never been to Chicago. I had never been anywhere! Surely I must be dreaming. Was it possible I might get to visit my Uncle Joe in Chicago?

I kept quiet as a mouse and just listened. I barely moved a muscle as the adults discussed the matter. I remembered well that children do not engage in adult conversation. If there was a chance that I might get to go to Chicago and visit my uncle, I was not going to do anything to stop that from happening. I'm proud to say

that even though I was well-behaved, from that moment on I was going to be the best little boy ever.

When my mother finally announced that we would indeed travel to Chicago on the train, I was dizzy with happiness. I could have jumped up and touched the ceiling. In bed that evening my face was sore from smiling. I had to pinch my cheeks to make sure I hadn't been dreaming. This would be my first train ride, my first trip to Chicago, my first big adventure. I was so excited I couldn't sleep. I was going to see my uncle Joe! This was more than I could ever have wished for.

There were many things to do to prepare for our trip. In the days that followed, I felt as if I were walking on air. Anything my mother asked me to do, I did—even before she finished asking! Mama and I rode the bus downtown to shop at the Black and White Store for a new shirt, a new pair of pants and a brand new pair of shoes. My uncle would be so proud when he saw how much taller I'd grown, and how good I looked in my new clothes.

But there was more to do when we got home. We weren't allowed to try on any of the clothes at the Black and White Store, including shoes, so Mama always did her best to buy the right sizes for me. I was happy the shoes fit just right, and that I didn't have to stuff wadded up newspaper to make them comfortable to wear. The pants, however, always needed some adjustments, so Grandmother carefully measured me and then set to work on the sewing machine to take them in at the waist and shorten the pant legs just a bit. In our neighborhood, it

was easy to find a tailor, but I was especially lucky because my grandmother was an expert at sewing.

Later that afternoon, Mama took me over to Mr. Sharp's house. Mr. Sharp was one of the neighborhood barbers who knew well how to deal with a young boy like me. It didn't take him long to administer the classic "bowl cut," which pretty much amounted to cutting my hair to the precise measurements of a bowl lying atop my black curls.

THE TRAIN RIDE TO CHICAGO

The day finally arrived for us to visit my Uncle Joe in Chicago. The excitement in my eyes and joy in my heart could barely be contained. When we got to the train station my grandfather helped us unload the car and take our bags to the train. We were traveling with one suitcase, a shoebox of sandwiches, fried chicken, a whole sliced pound cake, two containers, one filled with water and an empty one as well. I was so happy, I smiled from ear to ear. Nothing could dampen my spirits. I was really going to visit my uncle Joe!

The train had eight cars—the first one was the engine, and it was so big and loud I covered my ears as we boarded one of the passenger cars. "Mama, there's not much room

on this car," I complained, as I felt my first small prick of disappointment. She shot me a quick, hard look. "Boy, you told me you were going to be on your best behavior so you better just ride and be content." I glanced at my grandmother, who smiled faintly and rested a gentle hand on my shoulder as we searched for our seats. I suddenly remembered we were going to see my uncle in Chicago. I would have ridden on a cardboard box to get there to see him.

When we found our seats, they were small, and so *hard*. Everyone around us looked uncomfortable. We were packed in the train car so tight we could barely breathe. There was no room to stand up or move around. Sitting on my mother's lap, I saw people sitting on their suitcases, up and down the aisles. People stood in every inch of the train car. "Why is it so *crowded*?" I asked. My mother murmured to me in low tones it's because of our skin color. She said all dark-skinned people had to ride in this train car. She told me it was called "the colored car."

My mother's words left me confused, and once again my joy began to fade. I was disappointed and felt my heartache that we were being treated so badly, just because of our skin color. *Colored Car?* I'd never heard that phrase before and I whispered it into my lap. None of this made sense to a young boy on his first real adventure. I sat in silence as the train clattered down the track toward Chicago.

After a bit I became hungry, and I asked Mama if there was anywhere we could go to get something to eat. I desperately wanted to get up, stretch my legs, and eat somewhere comfortably. She reminded me about the shoebox of delicious food. Mama told me there were no accommodations for dark-skinned people—not even at most train stops. I heard the strain in her voice as she said, "You'll see, Sam. The signs read no coloreds allowed."

This information was also new to me. I couldn't figure out the logic behind it. Why hadn't my Uncle Joe told me about trains and the Colored Car? For the first time in my young life, I wondered what other information he and my mother may have hidden from me. I barely tasted the sandwiches Mama had so carefully prepared for us.

Soon, a new problem forced its way into my consciousness. I told my mother I had to use the restroom really bad. "That's what this empty container is for," she whispered. "In front of everyone?" I gasped in embarrassment. My eyes widened with shock. She nodded and replied, "Either this, or come with me and let me show you another way." I followed my mother as we bumped our way to the back of the train. "Excuse me, excuse me," she said, as we jostled between suitcases, crying babies and rows of standing bodies in the aisles. It took several minutes to reach to the back of the train car. There, she showed me a small closeted room containing a strange-looking dirty toilet seat sitting on a hole in the floor. As the unsteady door creaked open I saw the tiny

room was filled with swarming, angry flies. "This is the Colored Car's toilet," she stated grimly. I suddenly felt faint. The smell was so bad I began to gag. I clutched my stomach and threw up into the revolting hole. I had never seen *anything* so filthy, nasty and horrible. This was supposed to be a restroom? Instantly I understood the necessity of the empty container.

In a daze, I stumbled my way back to our seats. In my worst nightmare, I couldn't have imagined a place like this being called a restroom. I couldn't rid myself of that ghastly image and horrendous stench. My brain spun as I tried to fathom what we had done to deserve this mistreatment. I asked my mother why are we being treated like this? She said, "It's because we are dark-skinned people and this is the way that we are treated here in the South'. The explanation did not satisfy me, but for the time being, I let it go.

Later, I asked my mother for some water. She pulled out the pitcher of water she'd brought from home. By this time, I was not even surprised there was no water on the Colored Car to drink. Most of the train stops along the trip didn't have water fountains for colored people. Oh, there were nice, clean water fountains and restrooms at *every* stop for white passengers only. But, when we came to stops with water fountains for the colored car ticket-holders they were small, dirty and didn't look nearly as nice as the water fountains for white people. I told my

mother I didn't think this was fair or right. We shouldn't be *treated* like this!

Once again, Mama issued me that look of warning. "I'm only going to tell you this one more time, and I want you to listen carefully. Because of your skin color, you are *going* to be treated differently. I want you to remember that!" I still didn't understand, and I still didn't think it was right, but I nodded my head affirmatively. We were so close to seeing my Uncle Joe, I couldn't afford to mess up anything now.

At another one of the seemingly endless train stops, I got up to stretch my legs. Suddenly there was a commotion outside. I saw a young black man being forcibly removed from the train. In an instant, two policemen appeared and began to beat him with nightsticks. They placed him in handcuffs and drug him away. I was stunned, as I had never seen anything like that before. Was he a robber or an escaped convict I asked my mother? Mama did not answer my question and only later I learned he'd been arrested for trying to enter the train into a whites-only passenger door.

Once we got pulled into Cairo, Illinois, the conductor announced that coloreds were now free to move around the train. "Mama, did you hear what he said? He said coloreds can move around the train now!" I *so* wanted to look around and see the forbidden areas of the train I had been denied entry into. Once we crossed into Illinois we could move to other cars on the train. Illinois was a free

state; therefore, Jim Crow laws were not practiced. It was not segregated.

Mama knew I would not be satisfied until I had a look. We got up and again she said excuse me to people standing in the isles. Once more we stepped over luggage and shuffled through the narrow passage so that I could see the rest of the train. The white-only section of the train had spacious and comfortable seating. There were ample areas to place luggage and other personal items. It had nice, clean bathrooms. There was even a fine dining car where white passengers could get onboard meals. I inched slowly toward the dining car for a better look but there was a sign that said: "No Coloreds Allowed." My stomach rumbled with hunger as I peered into the glass door. "Mom, we can't go in the dining car?" She replied maybe on the train ride home from visiting your uncle.

SO GLAD TO SEE MY UNCLE

When we reached the station in Chicago, I looked out the window and I saw my uncle waiting for our arrival. He stood tall and dignified, and a flood of joy and relief and happiness swept over me. The grueling train ride and the indignities of the Colored Car was a disappointment that was temporarily forgotten. Tired and hungry we disembarked, and I ran to hug Uncle Joe. I looked forward to talking to him and spending time with him. There were so many questions I wanted to ask about my train ride experience and the Colored Car.

My mother and grandmother were also excited to see Uncle Joe. As they hugged, laughed, and talked I once again felt safe and protected in the company of my uncle.

"How was the trip?" he boomed over the sound of the noisy engines. I was suddenly shy and didn't want to tell him what I really felt. Everything was fine my mother said hastily. There were no problems she said as she looked at me. Uncle Joe beamed a big smile at us as he helped load our luggage into his Packard. On the way to his house, we stopped at a nice restaurant, and we ate a tasty meal. I hadn't realized how hungry I'd been. As we sat waiting for our food to arrive, I looked around cautiously for any signs warning people about who could eat there and who couldn't. I saw none. Was it possible the Colored Car had just been a bad dream? I looked at my mother, who was laughing and talking with animation. Was mama wrong about the Colored Car?

As my uncle drove us from the restaurant to his house, I marveled at the sights and sounds of Chicago. I had never seen so many buildings and so many people in a hurry. Everyone seemed busy with important things to do. My uncle's house was beautiful and spacious. It had five bedrooms, a library, and a sunroom. I even counted three and a half bathrooms. I had never seen such grandeur in my young life, and I swelled with pride as I realized that I—young Sam—was related to this wealthy, important man! Uncle Joe began to tell us of all the things we were going to do while visiting him in Chicago but my mind was so overwhelmed by the events of the day I could barely comprehend what he told us.

Later that evening my uncle and I went into the library to talk. I was finally able to unburden myself as I told him

of the ordeal we suffered on the train ride from Memphis to Chicago. I told him about the Colored Car and what we had endured. My words tumbled out as I described every detail, and how I now might have nightmares, and how my dreams for the future had been shattered by this train ride. When I finished talking, I was almost out of breath, as if something unseen was squeezing around my throat. I felt hot tears rising in my eyes and spilling down onto my cheeks.

Uncle Joe looked at me solemnly. He motioned for me to come sit close to him. He didn't speak right away, but when he did, it was with a gentle voice. As always, he had the right answers and the way to make even my worst experiences understandable. He explained that small-minded people will always try to make other people feel bad. "You don't want to waste your time dwelling on the ignorance of others," he explained. "Take your time, and learn who it is *you* want to be, and who is it you *don't* want to be." His words were simple but clear. There will always be people who will try to hold you back because you were born with dark skin, but it is *they* who are imprisoned by their own ignorance and fear. *You*, he told me, are destined to do whatever great things you want to do in this world. And that is a lesson you need to never forget.

It was getting late—way past my bedtime—and I was very tired. I think my uncle was tired too because his eyes were rimmed in red and his forehead had become furled. "Tomorrow we'll see the Science Museum," he said. "And the aquarium and Chinatown. I don't want to *explain* anything else to you about Chicago, I want to

show you, instead! Now, it's time for you to go to bed and get some rest."

Alone, in the bed at my uncle's house, I felt reassured and happy. I prayed for my uncle and my family, and I prayed that I would always remember to heed his words. Not everything in the world was fair, or as it should be, but maybe someday I would be one of those people who would change it for the better.

BIO

Reginald Floyd Smith, Sr. can usually be found around town speaking about and working toward equity, social justice and bettering the community. More often than not, the main topic of discussion is "race in America."

Reginald, a native of Memphis, Tennessee and was born during a turbulent time for Black People. He witnessed firsthand the injustices his people faced. Despite these obstacles, his faith and strong family upbringing gave him the strength he needed to survive. These factors contributed to the decision to devote his life to uplifting others.

After finishing Rust College in Holly Springs, Ms. Reginald experienced success in his professional life but felt something was missing. After years as a successful financial advisor and owning a childcare facility, he

decided to create a youth service organization to help at-risk youth. It was at this time Reginald began to understand the power of the experiences he had lived through and vowed to transfer the knowledge he possessed to the next generations.

Writing a book has always been on his bucket list, and The Colored Car is a fulfillment of his dream. He lives in Memphis, with his wife of 35 years and together they have two children.

Printed in the United States
By Bookmasters